Cognitive Psychology 2nd Edition

Connor Whiteley

DEDICATION
Thank you to all my readers for their continued support
without you I couldn't do what I love.

INTRODUCTION

Out of everything that psychology investigates, I think cognitive psychology has to be one of my favourites.

Whilst it is not as interesting as forensic psychology. Cognitive psychology is still great, and I love writing about it.

Since cognitive psychology is the subfield of psychology that focuses on the mind and how mental processes impact human behaviour.

From memory to how we think to emotion and more cognitive psychology investigates some fundamental aspects of our behaviour.

Because who are we if we can't remember?

I promise that's the only big question I ask in the book.

<u>Who is This Book For?</u>

That's a brilliant question.

Personally, I strongly believe this book is for anyone interested in learning more about cognitive psychology.

Whether you're a high school or university student, a trained psychologist or just someone wanting to learn about psychology. Then you should find this book very useful.

As it gives a great in-depth explanation of a wide range of cognitive psychology topics, all in an engaging and easy-to-understand way.

I promise this is not another boring psychology textbook!

<u>Who am I?</u>

Personally, I always love to know who the author is, so I know the information will be good.

In case you're like me, I'm Connor Whiteley, an author of over 30 books and 12 of which are psychology books. Their topics range from biological psychology to social psychology to the depths of Clinical psychology.

In addition, I'm the host of the weekly The Psychology World Podcast where you can listen to me talking about a range of psychology topics each week. Plus, I have the occasional guest. Including USA Today and New York Times Best-selling author J. F Penn.

Finally, I am a psychology student at the University of Kent, England.

Now that you know who I am, please read on to find out more about the amazing topic of cognitive psychology!

Cognitive Psychology 2nd Edition

PART ONE: MEMORY

CHAPTER 1: INTRODUCTION TO MEMORY

As I flick through my notes, I remember all the lectures, the good and the bad ones, as the information that I learned came back to me.

Even when I'm writing my sci-fi fantasy fiction, I am recalling and remembering inspirations and ideas.

So even with these two quick examples, you can see that memory is a vital part of our lives and if you search your day to day life then you are constantly learning information to remember it later.

Hence, the first section of this Cognitive Psychology book is dedicated to memory and how it works.

<u>The Basics of Memory:</u>

In its most basic form memory has three critical stages that information goes through and these are the core features of the models of memory that we'll look at later:

- Acquisition is the process of obtaining information and placing it into memory.
- Storage is the holding of the information in an enduring form in the mind.
- Retrieval- the point where we draw information to use in such a manner.

Acquisition:

When we learn information, this process of memory acquisition can be intentional or by accident, but in both these cases the learner or person is paying attention to the information and it is this intellectual engagement that is stored in the memory.

TIP: therefore, a possible tip is when you're revising or wanting to learn information try and be engaged in the material and that should help you. You can even fake your engagement if you need to.

Retrieval paths:

Another core feature of memory is the idea of retrieval paths as it is easier to remember information that is connected to other memories.

Therefore, when we retrieve information these connected memories can form retrieval paths.

This is similar to how the idea of memory palaces work.

However, more research is needed to explain how memory traces are represented in the brain.

For example, is there a physical mark in the brain because of these traces?

But evidence suggests that different areas of the brain store different parts of a memory. Such as touch, feel and emotion.

For instance, the different components of a fight; like the emotion; would be stored in another area than the pain.

Memory consolidation:

For a long-term memory to be formed, the memory must go through a memory consolidation process.

This is where new neural connections are made.

The need for consolidation can be found in cases where this process has been disrupted. Such as in cases of retrograde amnesia.

Memory retrieval:

As you will see in future chapters about memory, the ability to retrieve or remembering the information is vital and in terms of the retrieval of memories, it can sometimes fail completely or partially.

This can result in the 'tip of the tongue' effect.

However, whether or not a retrieval cue; something that helps you to remember the information; is helpful depends on if the cue created the context of the information learnt.

As a result of if it did then the individual could use the context's retrieval paths to retrieve the memory.

Forgetting:

Everyone forgets things and despite it being annoying and sometimes arguments can break out because we have forgotten something, many cases of forgetting can be simply understood as inadequate encoding. This is where the information never got into the memory in the first place.

As supported by fMRI data that shows differences in brain activity for information that was later remembered and later forgotten.

Generally, forgetting increases as the time since the information was acquired gets longer but the causes are still being debated.

One theory proposes that memory traces simply decay.

Another theory proposes that the production of new memories promote retrieval failure.

Inference can also result from the mixing together of memories.

These intrusions errors can be clearly seen in the misinformation effect were memories blur together.

Another type of memory error is when people correctly realise that an idea or concept is familiar, but they get it wrong about why it is familiar.

This is because familiarity and recollection are involved in two different memory systems.

Types of Memory:

As a final note on our introduction to memory, we'll have a quick look at the types of memory as it can be divided into two types:

- Explicit memory- conscious memory
- Implicit memory- unconscious memory

Furthermore, explicit memory can be broken down into:

- Episodic memory- remembering specific events
- Semantic memory- general knowledge

Whereas Implicit memory that is revealed by indirect tests can be broken down into

- Procedural- how to do something
- Priming- when because of having been exposed to one stimulus, this stimulus influences your response to the next stimulus.

- Perceptual learning- sensory systems improve through lived experiences.
- Classical conditioning- see a later chapter

Moreover, findings from healthy and brain-damaged people have shown a clear difference between explicit and implicit learning.

As a result, different areas of the brain activate for different types of learning.

The pre-frontal cortex for explicit learning.

The Striatum for implicit learning.

However, the relationship is complicated as the underlying systems for the explicit and implicit learning probably both interact with each other.

CHAPTER 2: RETRIEVAL OF MEMORIES

Focusing on the Long Term Memory, how do we remember things and how do we retrieve information that's stored in the Long Term Memory?

Importance of Context:

When it comes to retrieving memories the condition under which the memories was encoded is only one side of the story because memory performance is affected by the conditions we try to retrieve the memories under as well.

Context reinstatement:

The physical context has no effect on memory if the mental perspective doesn't change.

In fact, the physical setting only impacts memory indirectly and only if the physical setting helps us to recreate the setting in which the memory was encoded in. (Smith, 1979)

In other words, when the detectives take the victim back to the scene of the crime in TV Dramas. It probably doesn't do much to the victim's memory.

<u>Memory traces:</u>

These are important for the retrieval of information and the subsequent 'remembering' of information as memory traces are physical records of memories in the brain.

These are formed through maintenance rehearsal. This is where you keep rehearsing it and this keeps the information in the short-term memory for a while.

Although, this isn't very effective for transferring the information into the long-term memory.

In addition, you have elaborative rehearsals. This is when you think about the information continually and you associate it with things that are already known.

A common example of this is a memory palace.

<u>Levels of processing theory:</u>

Another theory or aspect of memory that increases the likelihood of you remembering something is the levels of processing theory.

This theory looks at whether greater activity in

processing leads to better memory.

For example, if you only read a list of words; shallow processing; then this leads to lower activity.

Whereas deep processing leads to higher activity. This is whether you read and imagine the words in the list in your mind.

Additionally, Laik and Lockhart (1972) found that after a delay. It's easy to remember the deep processing words.

Another level of processing is called: deepest processing meaning does the word you've trying to remember fit into the sentence. This links back to elaborative rehearsal.

For instance, if you need to memory the word: cat.

Then it's easier to remember the word in this sentence:

The cat ate the food.

Instead of the sentence:

The cat laid the eggs.

Self-reference:

Interestingly, Rogers et al (1979) found that words heard with a self-referencing question were remembered three times more likely to be remembered compared to words without the self-referencing.

The reason for this finding is because of a certain type of deeper processing.

As the self-referencing allows you to make connections with your own life. In return, this creates more retrieval cues.

Meaning you're more likely to remember the word *dog* when asked:

How's your dog today?

Compared to being asked:

What's that dog called again?

Multiple trace theory:

This theory proposes that we can make connections between multiple pieces of information. Giving us multiple memory traces as well as it gives us multiple ways to retrieve the word or information. (Retrieval paths)

Memory dysfunction:

It is a great shame that memory isn't perfect and that memory dysfunctions can occur. For example, amnesia means the loss of the ability to acquire or retain memories.

In addition, people who sadly suffer from retrograde amnesia have an inability to access old memories but an ability to form new memories.

Yet people who unfortunately suffer from anterograde amnesia can't form new memories.

CHAPTER 3: MULTI-STORE MEMORY MODEL

In psychology, there is a massive range of models to describe and explain how memory works and in the next two chapters, we're going to be exploring them in the first two steps on our cognitive journey.

But first- what is memory?

The definition is a cognitive process involving encoding, storing and retrieving information.

Yet I believe a more friendly definition is a mental process that involves the recording, storing and the retrieving of information about facts or an event.

All that retrieval means is when you bring that memory forward. In day to day life, we call this remembering something.

A typical example would be your partner telling you to buy some milk on the way home from work, simple but it will help.

Therefore, you encode the information that you need to get milk on the way home into your memory then you store that information in your memory throughout the day. Until you retrieve the information at home time as a reminder that you need to get milk.

Now that you hopefully understand what memory is. We can go into more depth about how it works…

The Multi-store memory model (MSM model):

This model was made up by Atkinson and Shiffrin (1968)

It's made up of three parts:

- The sensory memory- this is where information comes into the memory through our senses. Such as taste, touch, hearing, smell and sight. The amount of information that can be stored here (memory capacity) is unlimited, but this is probably because the information lasts here for a second, but in some cases, it can last for less than 200th of a second.
- The short-term memory (STM)- if the information is deemed important and you pay attention to it then it goes into the STM. Here the memory capacity is limited to about 6-8

pieces of information, but the information can stay here for a few minutes.

- Long term memory (LTM)- the MSM model believes that if the information is rehearsed enough and if enough attention is paid to it then it can end up here in the LTM. Here the memory capacity is unlimited, and it's proposed that the information can last a lifetime.

However, at each of these stages, the information is open to memory decay or displacement. Meaning that the information; in essences; is forgotten and doesn't get remembered.

In fact, when we say that we're forgotten information. Like: when one of our parents tells us to do someone and we 'forget' what's actually more likely is that the information never got encoded in the first place. In other words, it never entered our memory.

Critically thinking:

Before we move onto the studies supporting the model. Let's think about the model itself.

One good thing about the model is that it does explain memory well in a simple and easy to follow way.

Do you agree?

On the other hand, I believe that its simplicity is its

downfall because if the memory was that simple. We would all be memory experts.

But one of its other main faults is that it's built on the assumption that you need to rehearse/ repeat information for it to be stored in the LTM. However, how many times have we all read something once and be able to recall it. A few hours later without needing to reread or repeat it? I have and chances are we all have. Maybe not the reading example but probably something else. Like: what happens in a funny video or a conversation at work.

Let's move on the evidence for the model.

Bradley (1966):

Participants were given lists of words that were:

- acoustically similar (e.g. cat, mat)
- acoustically different (e.g. pen, cow)
- semantically similar (e.g. boat, ship)
- semantically different (e.g. book, tree)

Then their ability to remember (recall) the words were tested.

The results showed that in the STM there was a better recall of acoustically different than acoustically similar words

There were more errors with similar sounding words than distinctly sounding words

In addition, there was a slightly better recall of semantically different words than semantically similar words'

In conclusion, information is encoded acoustically because recall is affected by the sound of words in the STM.

Bradley (1966):

Participants were given the same lists of words in the previous experiment for STM and their recall of the words was tested

In LTM, no difference in recall of acoustically different and acoustically similar words.

The results showed much better recall of semantically different words than semantically similar words.

In conclusion, in the LTM, there is semantic encoding because recall is affected by the meaning of the word.

Critically thinking:

As both experiments were practically the same their evaluation will be done together.

Both experiments were potentially ecologically valid; how far can we apply the findings to the real world; because people do memory information by reading it either as a block of information; in a book; or in a list.

Equally, the study is generally low in ecological validity because how many people actually remember information from lists made up of words sounding and meaning similar and different things?

A more ecologically valid version of this experiment could possibly be the participants were asked to remember information from a textbook if they were a student, for example.

Summary:

The Multi-Store Memory model is a three-step model that explains memory as information that is repeated and given attention as it flows from the sensory memory, STM and LTM.

The first Bradley (1966) study showed that information is the STM is encoded according to sound.

Whereas the second study shows that information in the LTM is encoded according to meaning.

CHAPTER 4: WORKING MEMORY MODEL

Now that we've seen one way of how memory works, we're going to look at another model that goes into memory in more depth.

The Working Memory Model (WMM) was formulated by Baddeley and Hitch (1974) and it's made up of several sections.

But first Working Memory is memory that is temporarily activated so the information can be manipulated and applied to a specific problem.

Difference between the Short Term Memory and The Working Memory:

The difference is that the Working Memory involves you processing information differently than Short Term Memory as well as the Working Memory is Short Term Memory that is temporally active when it manipulates the information for a complex task.

The components of the Working Memory Model:

Central Executive:

This first section controls the memory and it allocates information to the subsections, as well as it deals with the task. Like: mental arithmetic and problem-solving.

Then you have the three subsections of the STM.

Visuospatial Sketchpad

This stores as well as processes information in a visual or spatial form.

Phonological Loop:

This section deals with spoken and written material and it's made up of two parts:

- Phonological/acoustic Store– this store is linked to speech and perception and it holds information in a speech-based form for a few seconds.

- Articulatory control process- this section is used to repeat and store verbal information from the phonological store.

Episodic buffer:

The last section is the episodic buffer this connects the Visuospatial sketchpad with the phonological loop.

Following being stored in the STM information can then be stored in the LTM if it doesn't get displaced or decay.

Critically thinking:

The model has great explanatory power as it allows us to explain a range of phenomena that can't be explained using the MSM model. For example the word length effect. This is a phenomenon where the capacity of the STM depends on the length of the word.

An example of this is trying to remember: Describe, discussing, catering, evaluating and Decomposing.

Compared to cat, dog, mat, gate and cook.

Which is easier to remember?

The list of short words should be.

However, as a result of the model's complexity, it's difficult to test scientifically. Especially, if you wanted to test all of the subsections in the model in the same experiment.

Saying that- let's look at some studies that have

managed to overcome that problem to some extent.

Working memory model- Conrad and Hull (1964)

Subjects were required to recall a list of letters. Some were phonologically similar, and others were different.

The lists containing the phonologically similar letters were harder to recall because the letters were easier to confuse with each other.

This supports the working memory model because it supports the idea of speech memory is stored in a sound-based system. This is now called the phonological store.

Baddeley (1996):

Subjects had to produce a random sequence of numbers by pressing a keypad.

Meanwhile, they were asked to complete one of three tasks:

- Recite the alphabet.
- Count numbers.
- Alternate between numbers and letters.

Results showed that randomness didn't change when counting or reciting. However, for alternating the randomness did decrease.

In conclusion, the switching between tasks is completed by a separate system. The central executive.

Critically thinking:

Both studies showed high internal validity as both studies measured what they intended to measure and they both supported the WMM.

Although, both studies only used participants from a western culture to support the model. Therefore, without further research how do we know that other cultures think in a similar way? And if they don't how do we know that their memory will support the model?

We will learn in the next book of the series that people from eastern cultures think differently from western cultures. Thus, is it possible that they could give these two experiments different results?

Who knows?

Summary:

The WMM is a model showing how memory works as information passes through the central executive were the information is given to one of the subsections: the phonological loop, episodic buffer or visuospatial sketchpad and ends up in the LTM.

Conrad and Hull (1964) shows that speech memory is

stored in a sound-based model.

Baddeley (1996) shows that switching between tasks involves another part of the memory.

CHAPTER 5: RELIABILITY OF MEMORY

When I first learnt about what's contained in this chapter, I found it really interesting because I had noticed that memory was obviously faulty and people changed the memory from what actually happened, but I didn't know why or what it was called. Thus, when I learnt why it was good to be able to explain to myself why other people's memories had changed so much.

Let's look deeper into this line of thinking. Let's say you're driving home and in reality, there was a car crash in front of you involving three cars. However, you remember there being four cars and 2 cyclists. Why?

Overall, many factors could be the reason why like:

- Post-event information- information about the event you're given after the event. This could be the reason because you overheard someone saying, "Thank god those two cyclists didn't get hit," it's a possibility.

- Misleading questions- this is were a question suggests information that isn't entirely true. For example: "How many cars were involved? Four?"

Nevertheless, the main theory involved in the reliability of memory is reconstructive theory. It's suggested that memory in the LTM isn't a passive process that stays the same as when the information is encoded. In fact, it could be an active recreation of the event every time we replay the event in our mind.

Additionally, the theory recognises that information that we encode during the event and after the event can; at least overtime; merge together to form a new memory to the point where we can't tell them apart anymore.

Hence, why we remember 4 cars instead of 3.

Loftus and Pickerel (1995):

This study suggests another reason why memory isn't reliability.

They asked family and friends about 3 childhood memories of the participants and if they had ever been lost in the mall. If the answer was yes, they weren't accepted into the study.

Then they sent a questionnaire through the post

containing the 3 memories and the lost in the mall memory.

They were asked to write as much as they could about the memory and rate how confident they were about the memory.

The results showed that 25% of people did believe the lost in the mall memory however they rated it as their least confident memory.

Overall, showing that memory can be unreliability as false memories can be created.

Critically thinking:

While the study shows that false memories can be created. It was only 25% of people and since it was done at home. The subject could have conferred with others.

Yuille and Cutshall (1986):

Although, memory can be reliable as demonstrated in this study where: 4 months after a gun store robbery were the owner was shot twice and killed. The researchers contacted the 21 witnesses and 13 of them signed up for the study.

They were asked to recall what happened during the robbery, then half of them were asked: did you see a blue panel on the getaway car? When it was yellow.

Then the other half was asked: did you were a broken headlight on the getaway car? When it wasn't.

Plus, they were asked where they afraid?

Results showed that they were 79%-84% accurate when compared to old police reports.

10 out of 13 recalled correctly the answer to their leading question.

While they weren't afraid, they did experience an Adrenaline rush.

Critically thinking:

The study has high ecological validity as this was a study involving a real event.

But as it was a one-off the results are unreproducible and unrepeatable. Although, the researchers could test other similar events to see if the results could be simpler.

Summary:

The main reason why memory can be unreliable is because of reconstructive theory.

Loftus and Pickerel (1995) shows our memory can be unreliable because of false memories.

Whereas Yuille and Cutshall (1995) shows us that memory can be reliable as the witnesses were 79%-

84% correct when compared to police reports.

CHAPTER 6: EMOTION AND MEMORY

It sounds interesting, doesn't it?

How can emotion possibly affect our memory?

Impossible right?

Wrong- our emotions can and does affect our memory.

In this chapter, we're going to be discussing the special memory mechanism that creates vivid and highly detailed recordings of the event when the witnessing or receiving of the news of the event is unexcepted and is emotionally arousing.

That mechanism is called a flashbulb memory.

Before we go into detail about how it works. Let me tell you an example.

The most famous example of a flashbulb memory is a person's memory of the 9/11 terror attack in 2001. If you're old enough to remember the attack; which I'm not; then you probably remember hearing about the attack in clear detail.

That is because the event was unexcepted and you got emotionally aroused.

Now we have a point of reference to explore the idea. We can go into the theory itself.

The theory of flashbulb memories was formed by Brown and Kulik (1977).

They state for flashbulb memories to be formed there are two mechanisms.

The formation mechanism- for the memory to be formed the event needs to be unexcepted and it needs to be of personal consequences. (emotionally arousing) if these conditions have been met then a photographic version of the event is imprinted in the memory.

The maintenance mechanism- once the event has been imprinted in the memory it needs to be maintained. Maintenance is achieved through overt rehearsal and covert rehearsal.

Overt rehearsal is when you discuss the event with other people.

Covert rehearsal is when you replay the memory in your own mind.

Going back to the 9/11 example, the terror attack creates flashbulb memories because the attack was very unexpected because who would except terrorists to fly planes into buildings killing thousands of innocents in one day?

Then it's emotionally arousing because the attack affected everyone, and it practically stopped the world and it was the beginning of increased security and much conflict resulted from that attack.

As a result of those factors, a flashbulb memory is formed.

Now you know how a flashbulb memory is created. We'll look at some evidence for it.

Neisser and Harsch (1992)

On the morning after the Challenger disaster, 106 university students were given a questionnaire at the end of their introductory psychology class and were told to answer questions. Like: how did you hear about the disaster?

2 and a half years later, they were given the questionnaire again and asked: how confident they were about their memories and if they had done the questionnaire before. Only 25% of the subjects said yes.

With there being a lot of mistakes with the reports,

semi-structured interviews were completed using retrieval cues to see if the subjects would refer to the report, they wrote a few months ago or the original days.

At the end of the interview, they were shown their original reports.

To give the reports a score the researchers looked at 7 content questions.

Results showed, that there were a lot of differences between the two reports however the subjects were very confident about their answers.

This links to flashbulb memories as they show that even though we think that the memories are actual and vivid. In reality, they aren't.

Critical thinking:

It's a positive of the study that it used more than one method; they used questionnaire and interviews; to improve their finding and credibility.

However, as this was a one-off this can't be repeated but to increase credibility the same study should be done using other events to test the reliability of the results.

Sharot et al (2007):

The study was some 3 years after the 9/11 terror attack.

The sample was made up of 24 new Yorkers who were present on the day of the attack. Subjects were put into an fMRI.

When put into the fMRI there were cues. These cues were a word was associated with the summer or September of 2001 which was projected alongside, so the subject would link the word to the attack or the summer.

Brain activity was observed throughout. The personal events of the summer served as a baseline for evaluating the attack memories.

Afterwards, they were asked to rate the vividness of their memories, detail and the confidence of the memories.

Only half of the subject reported having flashbulb memories and they were closer to the world trade centre.

Results showed that people who were closer to the world trade centre on the day of the attack had higher activation of the amygdala compared to the previous summer. Other participants had equal activation when thinking of the attack and the summer.

People who had flashbulb memories had higher activation as well. Suggesting that close personal experience of the attack may be critical in engaging a neutral mechanism for the production of flashbulb memories.

Critically thinking:

While the study effectively managed to show a biological basis for this special mechanism for remembering events. It was a quasi-experiment. This is a type of experiment that doesn't have a clear independent variable; the thing you change in your experiment; and a clear dependent variable; the thing that changes because of the independent variable; so if a follow up study was performed using this experiment then it should be done with a clear independent variable and dependent variable.

An example of the new possible variables is:

- The location of the participant related to how far they were from the towers.
- The level of activation in the amygdala.

Summary:

A flashbulb memory is a special type of memory mechanism that occurs when an event is unexcepted and of personal consequence.

Neisser and Harsch (1992)- shows us that flashbulb

memories can be unreliable.

Sharot et al (2007)- shows us that there is a biological basis for flashbulb memories.

PART TWO: DECISION-MAKING, THINKING AND TECHNOLOGY

CHAPTER 7: DECISION-MAKING AND THINKING

Entering our next section of this Cognitive Psychology book, we're going to be investigating how we think and make decisions.

Because let's face it sometimes humans make great decisions but other times, we make some pretty stupid decisions.

But why do we differ so much in our decision making?

That is the focus of this next section.

Mental Representations:

Firstly, thinking is the operations that we apply to mental representations; meaning when we think about something. We are taking the mental image or representation and applying it.

In addition, mental representations are the contents of the mind and these representations; for lack of a better term; represent objects, events, and states of fairs in the mind.

Resulting in these representations being used in our thinking because it's the idea of the event or object that matters and not the physical entity.

Example:

I know that this idea of mental representations as well as thinking is complex. Therefore, let's use an example.

So, let's say that I was thinking about a fight earlier so I would have the memory of the fight in my mind. This is the mental representation.

Subsequently, as I think about the event, I can apply the thinking process to the mental representation of the fight. Hence, I might replay it in slow motion to understand what happened or do something else.

However, the key takeaway is that I have the mental representation of the fight in my head and I apply thinking to the representation.

Resulting in me thinking about the event.

Types of Representations:

Although, these mental representations can be split into two very important types. Such as the analogical representation shows us the physical characters of the represented object. Like, a guitar or a book.

Whereas, the symbolic representation doesn't represent what it is meant to. For example, the word 'cat' does represent the animal 'cat' in the physical sense.

Interesting, in the brain, all these representations are encoded in a shared brain area.

Additionally, Kosslyn, Pascual-Leone, Felican, Camposano, Keenan et al (1999) found when transcranial magnetic stimulation is used it disrupts the visual cortex. Meaning they struggled with sight but they struggled with visualizing mental images as well.

Suggesting that mental representations are formed or involve the same brain areas as real visual images.

Direct thinking:

This type of thinking occurs when we're thinking about a goal and the process of our thoughts depends on what we are trying to achieve. For example:

- Reasoning

- Judgement
- Decision making
- Problem-solving

Heuristics:

I'm dedicating a whole chapter to heuristics and thinking biases in the next chapter but it makes sense to introduce the topic now.

Therefore, heuristics are a strategy for making a quick judgement, at the price of occasional mistakes and the term is taken from computer science to mean a shortcut method for getting results.

One of these types of thinking error is called the representative heuristic. This is a strategy to judge whether an individual or thing is representative of a whole category.

For example, if one man or woman represents all men and women.

Finally, the availability heuristic is a strategy for judging how frequently something happens or how common it is based on how easily examples come to mind. This judgment can may leave us with a distorted way of some social relationships.

Theories of Thinking:

Utility theory:

Every decision has its own benefits; things that bring us closer to our goals; and costs. These are things that move us further away from our goals.

Therefore, the theory proposes that we make decisions based on a cost/benefits analysis that is subjective to our perceptions of these costs and benefits.

However, this theory assumes that people have unlimited knowledge, time and information processing.

Too many options:

Surely humans prefer to be spoiled for choice when it comes to making a decision as this would allow us to make the best possible choice for yourselves, wouldn't it?

However, it turns out that humans prefer to have many choices but we are more likely to make a choice when we have fewer options.

For example, Iyengar & Lepper (2000) found people were more satisfied when they had only 6 options compared to 24 to 30 options.

In addition to us being happier when we have fewer

options to choose from, the way we make our choice is more important to our happiness compared to the outcome.

Whilst, this seems to show that people would prefer to make decisions that don't lead them towards their goal.

It may be better to evaluate decisions based on the process because people prefer decisions they can explain.

Therefore, it may not lead to a better outcome but people may be more satisfied by rating a decision about the process rather than the outcome.

CHAPTER 8: BIASES IN DECISION-MAKING

This is another area of interest for me not for personal reasons, but I just find it interesting how thinking can be faulted.

One of the many models of thinking was proposed by Kahneman (2003) this is system 1 and 2 thinking. It's two hypothetical ways of thinking.

System 1 thinking is fast, instinctive and automatic. While this way of thinking is good and needed sometimes it comes at the cost of not being rational or accurate.

An example of this type of thinking is if you were driving past someone who was being attacked. Would you help or not?

Another could be if you're going to go on a date with someone and they asked you in person.

System 2 thinking is slower, more logical and conscious thinking. This is good when we have time to think about a problem or something in detail.

For example, where to go on holiday or what brand of cereal you like.

However, we will be looking at two factors that can cause a bias in how we think.

The first is the Peak-end rule. This is where we only tend to remember the most interesting part of the event and the end.

For instance, let's say you were out with family having amazing food and a great time but in the middle of the evening another group of people were picking on your parents for any reason and they caused a massive fight and ended up getting kicked out. This would be the peak.

Then you go back to having a great evening full of laughter and great food. However, at the end of the evening, your Grandma causes a minor argument with your parents because she wants to take a detour on the way home to get some milk, but your parents just want to go home so she kicks up a fuss. This would be the end.

So overall it was an okay evening and probably a good evening out as you had amazing food and family with only two problems.

But chances are that you would say the evening was bad because you would memory the evening due to of the most interesting bit and end of the evening and not take in the rest of the evening into consideration.

Hence, the peak-end rule is bias.

Kahnemann (1993):

Subjects were asked to put one hand in painfully cold water. While on the other hand, they recorded how they felt. 1 was no pain. 5 was extreme pain.

There were two conditions- the first they placed their hands in the cold water (14 degree Celsius) for 60 seconds.

Condition two- the same as condition 1 but they kept their hands in the water for another 30 seconds while value was opened with warm water. Rising the temperature by a degree.

Subjects were told to do another trial and that they could choose the condition that they would do.

Results showed that 80% of subjects preferred to do condition 2 again because of that slight decrease in pain towards the end.

<u>Critically thinking:</u>

While the study was effective at showing how the peak-end rule was a thinking bias. It's low in ecological validity as not many people would have to decide about what bowl to put their hands in.

Nevertheless, a way how to make the findings more creditable would be to perform interviews with the participants to see why they choose the condition they did and see if it was because of the peak-end rule.

<u>Tversky and Kahneman (1981):</u>

Another thinking bias is called: the framing effect. This is where there is bias in your thinking about a decision involving risk because of the framing of the solution in terms of the positive outcomes and negative outcomes. As demonstrated in this experiment.

The experiment used 307 US undergraduate volunteer students.

Subjects were given a scenario about the USA being infected by a strange Asian virus and it was excepted to kill 600 people.

Then people were given the information about programs to help with the outbreak for some the information was framed positively and others negatively.

The programs in condition 1 were: A- 200 people will be saved.

B- 1/3 chance that 600 will be saved. 2/3 chance that 600 will die.

For this condition, 72% of people chose program A.

Condition 2- program C- 400 people will die.

D- 1/3 chance no one will die and 2/3 chance that 600 people will die.

For this condition, 78% chose program D.

All the programs are effectively the same.

Results showed that when information is phrased positively people tend to choose a certain outcome and avoid the chance of uncertainty.

However, in terms of a negative frame about people dying. People tend to go towards the uncertainty about the chance that people could live.

Critically thinking:

Overall, the study had strong internal validity as it did measure what it intended to. Which was how thinking is influenced by the framing of the problem.

However, it has low ecological validity as no one

would really never have to decide this, would you?

Therefore, to add credibility to the findings focus groups could be done to explore the reasons why people choose what they did, so they could see if the thinking bias actually played a role. Or if the experimenters linked the findings to the bias because they wanted there to be a link.

Summary:

System 1 thinking involves quick and unconscious thinking.

System 2 thinking involves logical and conscious thinking.

The peak-end rule is where your thinking about an event based on the most interesting part and the end of the event.

The framing effect is the bias involved when we make a decision involving risk based on the framing of the problem.

Kahneman (1993) shows us how the peak-end rule can affect decision making.

Tversky and Kahneman (1981) shows us how the framing of the problem can affect our thinking.

CHAPTER 9: DECISION NEUROSCIENCE

After looking at decision making, thinking and biases in thinking our last topic will focus on Decision neuroscience. This is an area of research that focuses on the brain and how it impacts decision making.

As we have already learnt a lot of things can influence our decisions. For example:

- The social situation
- Strategy
- Pattern recognition
- Emotional (referred to as a gut feeling)

Neuroeconomics:

Traditionally, decision making was investigated by economics as economics needed psychology to make better decisions as well as psychology needed economics to take advantage of the normative framework.

However, both psychology and economics need neuroscience. To find out the more gradualate information; the biological information to gain a better insight into decision making.

Consequently, the rather novel discipline of decision neuroscience or neuroeconomics was made to integrate neuroscience, psychology and economics methodologies to develop better and more accurate models of decision making.

Additionally, in order to develop these models decisions, neuroscience looks at the brain-behaviour associations that are relevant for decision making as well as neural correlates related factors that influence our decisions making.

Emotion and decision making:

As humans, we are constantly making decisions based on our emotions. For instance, who we love, what we do amongst other things as well as this emotional decision making is commonly referred to as a gut feeling.

This involves all other processes that don't involve rational thinking and these include the following:

- Emotional and automatic processing
- Conscious "gut" feeling

- Unconscious processes

Interestingly, different brain areas are involved in these emotional processes when compared to the brain areas that are involved in the more rational decision-making processes.

In these processes, two brain areas that are involved are the amygdala; as some decisions are driven by fear of punishment; and the striatum. As some decisions are driven by reward.

Additionally, the ventromedial prefrontal cortex (vmPFC) is a brain area that recalls and uses these reactions to drive future behaviour.

For example, if I was deciding on an investment where I was fearful of losing a large amount of money then my amygdala could be more active, as well as my decisions about this investment would be used to guide my behaviour in future investment situations.

Linking to this fact, according to Rilling et al (2003) cooperation leads to higher activation of the striatum and orbitofrontal cortex and the strength of the activation can predict future cooperation.

Hence, showing the importance of brain regions in decision making in the present and future.

Whereas, the dorsolateral prefrontal cortex (dlPFC) is a brain area that is considered crucial for self-control and it communicates with the vmPFC. (McClure et al, 2004)

In terms of decision making, this brain area helps us to make decisions that involve self-control. For example, if you want to buy a very expensive item.

<u>Game theory:</u>

In its simplest form, Game Theory can be described as a series of scenarios and ultimatums that give us different behaviours, as well as Game theory, gives us several experimental scenarios.

For ultimatum games, it's predicted that humans will always accept the offer but in reality, 50% of the time people reject the offer, so proposes to make fairer offers.

<u>Social influences:</u>

As previously mentioned, social factors constantly influence our decisions because of factors like ingroup conformity as well as selfish or altruistic motivations. All influence us when we make decisions.

For example, in my <u>Psychology of Human Relationships</u> book, I talk about Bystanderism and ingroup conformity plays a massive role in deciding whether to help a person in need.

Social motivations and emotion:

These are motivations that come from social and societal factors and these social motivations are strongly linked to positive and negative emotions.

Furthermore, in many situations, social norms have more weigh than personal gain. Like: money.

In addition, some research found that irrationality comes from the involvement of anger, guilt, shame and rewards from revenge.

CHAPTER 10: COGNITION IN A DIGITAL WORLD

Welcome to the last stage of our cognitive journey and I've saved the best for last for you.

I welcome you to one of the most hotly contested topics of our time.

Is technology bad for us?

How is technology affecting us?

Is technology bad for children?

And yes, it would be wonderful if there was one answer, but technology is good and bad.

Before I share our two main studies for these chapters. I'll quickly flick over some other studies that show the effects of technology on our mental processes. As there's no real theoretical information to share.

Except that we know that our experience of the world shapes our neuronal connections in our brain because of neuroplasticity. (See the first book in the series for more information)

However, as more and more of humanity is becoming exposed to technology it's reasonable to assume that mental processes could change as a result of this increase.

Key studies:

Rosser et al (2007) found that surgeons who played first-person video games were faster and more accurate in surgery simulations.

Sanchez (2012) showed that playing first-person video games and other technology that requires spatial abilities could help students to understand abstract scientific concepts.

Rosen and Cheever (2013) showed that students who surrounded themselves with more technology while studying scored lower average grades than others.

And there are many more interesting studies but now we'll focus on two other key studies.

Sparrow et al (2001):

This study looks at the concept of transferable memorable. This is; in essences; when people don't bother remembering the information themselves and decide to store the information in other stores. Like other people or a computer.

For instance, you don't bother remembering your friend's birthday because your partner knows when it is. Oh, believe me it sounds bad but I had a friend who did that.

Subjects were asked to type 40 trivia facts into a computer. Some facts were new, and others were common knowledge.

As a 2x2 independent sample design, the four conditions were: the first group was told that their information would be saved then half of that group was told to remember the information, the second was told that the information would be erased after typing it in and then half of that group was told to remember the information.

Results showed that being asked to remember the information made no significant difference between the groups.

However, knowing if the information would be erased or not did.

	Asked to remember	Not asked
Save information	19%	22%
Erased information	29%	31%

In conclusion, people who believed that they could retrieve the information from the computer later made far less effort to remember the facts.

Critically thinking:

The study effectively measures what it intended to, and it addresses a modern issue. Giving it both internal validity and temporal validity. (how valid the findings are in relation to time)

Since they aren't able to measure the effort level in this study, we can't tell why this difference exists. So, if the study was to be redone I would suggest completing semi-structured interviews so the researchers could investigate how much effort everyone put into remembering the facts.

Fery and Ponserre (2001):

They studied 62 right-handed people with no golfing experience.

They were split into three groups: control, learning group; people who wanted to improve their golfing skills; and the entertainment group. People who wanted to play golf for fun and engaged with a golf simulator.

Results showed that putting improved in the learning and entertainment group. Most significant in the learning group.

In conclusion, for stimulation to be useful they need to be reliable by showing demonstrations of putting and there has to be motivated to improve and learn.

Critically thinking:

The study uses a large sample size, so this adds reliability to the findings as the same behaviour is shown by a number of people.

However, the study wasn't a cross-cultural study so we can't say if this behaviour is universal and if other cultures would show the same results.

A possible reason for this is that a culture that is unfamiliar to technology or has limited access to it could possibly not show the same results if the study was repeated using them.

Summary:

Rosser et al (2007) found that surgeons who played first-person video games were faster and more accurate in surgery simulations.

Sanchez (2012) showed that playing first-person video

games and other technology that requires spatial abilities could help students to understand abstract scientific concepts.

Rosen and Cheever (2013) showed that students who surrounded themselves with more technology while studying scored lower average grade points than others.

Fery and Ponserre (2001) found that technology can be used to improve skills.

Sparrow et al (2001) shows us that technology can cause us to become lazy and forget information.

CHAPTER 11: LEARNING: HABITUATION AND THE BASIS OF LEARNING

Learning is a great ability that animals have as learning aids us in survival as well as it allows us to broaden our minds to learn great things about the world around us.

Also, I love learning, so I was always going to be interested in this next section of the book.

You can define learning as an adaptive process where you create associations as a result of experiences that you remember.

Habituation:

The simplest form of learning could be habituation. This is a decision in the responsiveness to a stimulus once the stimulus has become familiar.

The benefit of habituation is that we need to pay

attention to unfamiliar stimuli as these could be dangerous or threats.

Therefore, we use habituation so we can ignore familiar inputs that are found to be inconsequential and instead we focus on the novel ones.

A personal example is during my first year of university I lived in campus accommodation and there was a very annoying banging sound whenever the radiator was on and we didn't control when the radiator was on or off.

However, over time I stopped noticing the banging because I knew that it wasn't a threat, so I learned that I didn't need to respond to the stimulus of the sound.

Then you have dishabituation this is an increase in responsiveness when something novel is no longer present following a series of pre-sensation of something familiar.

For example, you tend to automatically notice when the humming of your fan stops in the summer.

This is important as a change in stimulation can bring new information about the world.

Like: when a bird stops singing, then has it has been killed by a predator? If so, then a group of deer would like to know.

The problem with habituation is that it only provides us with information about a single stimulus.

Although, in the next chapter we will investigate more complex forms of learning.

Neural basis of learning:

If you've read Biological Psychology, then you know that I love the topic of Neuroplasticity and this concept is very useful as when we learn new information. This can cause the brain to remap itself according.

Other ways that we learn using our brains include:

- Presynaptic facilitation- a process that underlies many kinds of learning. This occurs when learning results in an increased release of neurotransmitters into the synapse.
- Long term potentiation- a long-lasting increase to the neuron's response to specific input caused by repeated stimulation.

The reason why this is referred to as 'long term' is because this lasting increase can last for days or even weeks, as well as it a potentiation because the mechanism involves an increase in neurons firing potential.

- Shaping is the process were through some encouragement or coaching you can elicit the desired response by rewarding behaviours that increasingly similar to the response.

Such as:

- Mouse goes near the lever.
- Reward
- Mouse faces the lever
- Reward
- Mouse has their evaluated
- Reward
- Mouse reaches lever
- Reward
- Mouse touches lever
- Experiment begins

I know that it's a long-winded process but it's one of the only ways to get a mouse or rat to cooperate!

Biological Basis of Learning:

There are biological constraints on learning because all species are deposited to form some associations and not others.

This is most probably a direct product of our evolutionary past. (Rocin and Kaltz, 1971; 1972)

Building upon evolution's impact further, taste aversion is a type of classical conditioning and it's an example of prepared learning.

- Prepared learning- learning that occurs with extensive training because of an evolved predisposition to the behaviour.

Prepared learning can be demonstrated is instrumental conditioning because according to the animal viewpoint some rewards and responses go together, and others do not. (Shettleworth, 1972)

Tuning the laws of learning can be important because as the above research has shown whilst some laws are considered general laws, some need to be tuned as some animals can learn associations with ease and others with difficulty and others, not at all.

For example, the Clark's Nutcracker can remember the location of thousands of pine nut caches over the area of a few square miles. This few of us humans could ever achieve.

This memory is likely to be an evolutionary adaption.

CHAPTER 11: TYPES OF LEARNING
How do we learn?

This is a fundamental question about human existence in my opinion because if we didn't learn then we would soon die or injury ourselves.

One example is that if we never learned the relationship between fire and pain. I think it's fair to say that we would soon burn to death or be in constant pain as we constantly touched the flames.

Classical conditioning:

This learning provides us with the information about the relationships that exists in the world, and it can be defined as a form of learning where one stimulus is paired with another so the organism can learn the relationship between them.

In classical conditioning, you have the famous Pavlov study.

In short, this study looked at the conditioning of dogs and the relationship between their food bowl being present and the dog's salivation.

Please note, whilst the information in the next few paragraphs may sound complex there is a shorter, simpler explanation afterwards.

Moreover, in classical conditioning, you have several key responses and stimuli. Such as:

- Unconditioned response (UR)- a response elicited by an unconditioned stimulus without prior training.
- Unconditioned stimulus- a stimulus that reliably triggers a particular response without prior training.
- Conditioned response- a response elicited by an initially neutral stimulus (the conditioned stimulus) after it has been paired with an unconditioned stimulus.
- Conditioned stimulus- an initially neutral that comes to elicit a new response due to a pairing with the unconditioned stimulus.

Simpler Explanation:

In simpler terms, classical conditioning works on any responsive animal and it occurs when you have a neutral stimulus that does not elicit a response.

For example, a green light wouldn't cause you to do

anything. Except, maybe wonder why the hell there's a green light.

Then during learning, you give a neutral stimulus meaning and after learning the conditioned stimulus this stimulus elicits a conditioned response.

For example, the green light could mean that your dinner is ready.

Can Classical Conditioning be Undone?

Classical conditioning can be undone through the process of extinction.

This is the weakening of a learned response that is produced if a conditioned stimulus is now repeatedly present without the unconditioned stimulus.

In other words when you forget the association between the CS and CR.

Although, this extinction can be temporary as spontaneous recovery can occur. This is the reappearance of an extinguished response after an interval in which no further trials conditioning has been presented.

An example of this is when sleep you have some spontaneous recovery because of memory consolidation.

This is why after exposure therapy ends people often

relapse. Hence, the need for follow up after exposure therapy ends.

Operant conditioning:

Moving onto our next type of learning, the main difference between operant conditioning and classical conditioning is that in operant conditioning the behaviour is voluntary but in classical conditioning, the behaviour isn't. For example, salivation is automatic- and you can use this conditioning for animal training.

Nonetheless, operant conditioning like most things in psychology has its own special list of terminology. Including:

- Positive reinforcement- when you give them something good.
- Positive punishment- give them something bad
- Negative reinforcement- when you take away something good.
- Negative punishment- take away something bad.

Furthermore, as you're trying to teach or learn a voluntary behaviour in this type of conditioning it can be used for children.

However, when it comes to children you are encouraged to do positive reinforcement for children and if you have to use negative punishment.

Compared to the more punitive and not recommended and sometimes just cruel, positive punishment and negative reinforcement.

In fact, in operant conditioning, there are a number of other ways to reward and punish people in order to elicit the voluntary behaviour.

For example, you can use partial reinforcement; reinforcement for some behaviour; and a ratio schedule. This is when a reward occurs after a set number of responses. Like: you get to go to Disneyland after cleaning your bedroom 20 times perhaps.

Equally, you could use an Interval schedule to reward someone, because in this schedule the rewards occur after a set period. Such as: cleaning your room after 6 months.

Learning in the real world:

So far we've looked at classic and operant conditioning, but what real-world applications are there for conditioning?

Well, believe it or not, conditioning has a lot of beneficial impacts in the real world. For example taste aversion.

This is an association between the taste of food with

the symptoms of gastrointestinal illness, as well as an example of aversion therapy is alcoholism.

Although, a negative of conditioning is called learned helplessness. This is a condition of passivity apparently created by exposure to aversive event or conditions that inhibit or prevents learning in later situations that are avoidance or escape is possible.

Observational learning:

If you're read Sociocultural Psychology, then you would know that I truly love Observational Learning also known as Social Cognitive Theory. Due to this theory can be applied to so many different situations. Like: learning.

Social cognitive theory:

In short, this theory proposes that we learn behaviours by watching others and these others are called: models.

In addition, the model's behaviour is more likely to be followed if:

- The model is competent
- Has power or prestige (like a parent)
- Behaviour is relevant

Although, a model is only effective if they get the attention of the watcher and if the watcher is motivated to learn the behaviour as well as if they encode the information, so they know how to perform the behaviour.

Finally, Observation Learning is important and plays a vital role in each of the following types of learning:

- Generalisation is the tendency for a stimulus that is similar to the conditioned stimulus to elicit a response that is similar to the learnt response.

For example, if you conditioned someone to be scared of a cat then it's possible that they would become scared of a dog. As both animals are furry with four legs and a tail.

- Discrimination is an aspect of learning in which the organism learns to respond differently to stimuli that they associate with the unconditioned stimulus.
- Instrumental conditioning is a form of learning were the participant receives a reinforcer the desired action, so they learn the response and the reinforcer.

The law of effect is that Thorndike's theorised that a response followed by a reward would be strengthened whereas a response followed by no reward or punishment will be weaker.

CHAPTER 12: SCHEMA

Now we're onto one of my favourite bits of cognitive psychology: schema theory!

Now I do have a personal interest in schema theory because it affected a friendship of mine as a child because a lot of people had a schema about this person and that well as I'll explain in a minute affect their thinking and perceiving information about this person.

Anyway- enough of the story onto the science.

A schema is a framework or concept that affects the way we encode, interrupt and retrieve information.

The way how schema influences memory will be clearer as we explore the studies but there are three types of schema:

- Social schemas- these are mental representations of a group of people. These include stereotypes.
- Scripts- mental representations of a sequence of events.
- Self-schema- mental presentations about ourselves.

Bartlett (1932):

Bartlett got participants to read a Native American story called: War of the Ghosts. Then he got them to recall as much as they could from the story. They did this serval times.

Bartlett found that the accounts were distorted in serval ways:

- They were rationalised- subjects made the story read more like an English story.
- Levelling- leaving out information that wasn't essential to the story.
- Changes in order- reordering the story to make it more coherent.
- Sharping- filing in the blanks with details.

As a result of the study not being well controlled therefore half of these mistakes could have been down to conscious guessing rather than schema influenced events.

Critically thinking:

While the study did manage to show how memory affects the encoding and retrieval of memory.

The study wasn't well controlled so half of these mistakes could have been down to conscious guessing rather than schema influenced events.

As a result, a follow-up study should be done with clear instructions to participants so that more of these mistakes can be erased.

Daley and Gross (1983):

They got two groups to watch the same video of a girl doing a school test.

One group was led to believe she had a low Socioeconomic (SES) background.

One other group believed she had a high SES background.

Then they were asked to rate her performance.

The group that believed she was from a high SES believed she would be better.

In conclusion, SES related schemas play a role in interpreting ambiguous social situations.

Critically thinking:

The study has high internal validity as it effectively shows that schema does play a role in ambiguous social situations.

However, the study lacks ecological validity because how many people would be asked to rate a girl's performance based on a video in the real world?

Would a more ecologically valid scenario be to meet and interact with someone that was dressed in a way stereotypically of High or low SES background and then ask the participant to say whether or not they believe that they would do well in a school test?

Just a thought.

Summary:

A schema is a network or framework that influences how we encode, interrupt and retrieve information.

Bartlett (1932) shows that schema can influence memory as it caused the memory of the story to change for the participants.

Darley and Gross (1983) shows us that our schema of a group of people can influence our interruption of events.

PART FOUR: SOCIAL COGNITION, EMOTION AND CONSCIOUS

CHAPTER 13: INTRODUCTION TO SOCIAL COGNITION

Humanity's ability to think, interact, form communities and do other things as a group is rather remarkable compared to other animals. As it is this ability of humanity's that has allowed it to accomplish so much.

But how are we able to do this group work and working together?

Well, this is where our next topic comes in as social cognition looks at the mental processes behind our social interactions and group processes.

Although, it must be stated upfront that primates have unusually large brains for our body size, and this comes with the price of very high energy costs.

Meaning that to compensate for this high energy costs, there must be a good explanation for why we have this large organ that costs us so much energy.

Evolutionary:

Our social cognition can be explained by evolutionary theory because our large brains aided our survival as they allowed us to develop social skills. That allowed us to form groups and communities that was beneficial for the survival of the species. As this allowed us to hunt in packs, share the workload and aid in the survival of the species in other ways,

Ecological hypothesis:

This hypothesis looks at the reason for our big brains from an environmental standpoint and the hypothesis proposes that our big brains are a bi-product of cognitive demands of certain behaviours. Like: foraging mental maps of the landscape (for example), innovation and tool use.

As a result, these instrumental skills gave us a direct advantage over living as individuals for survival.

Therefore, we developed better foraging skills amongst other skills as we could forage in groups and learn from others.

Social learning:

Personally, I have always loved social learning theory as it's always useful and interesting to consider.

Therefore, applying social learning theory to Social Cognition, our large brains reflect the social skills that developed through social competition, and in order to achieve success socially, we needed to develop skills. Such as deception, forming alliances and manipulation.

Meaning that social skills gave a direct advantage to the individual to survive.

Thus, having and being able to use social skills is beneficial to the individual and not only the species.

CHAPTER 14: EMPATHY

A key feature of being human is to have empathy as this allows us to be kind to others and empathy is a very important skill to have in order to navigate the social world.

However, the definition of empathy isn't straightforward, because how do you define empathy?

I suppose a simple definition would be: the identification and sharing of an emotional or affective state.

Although, this makes empathy sound a bit too simple as well as this definition is far too board.

Therefore, if you used this definition then you could mistake other mental states as empathy. As you will see later.

Consequently, the requirements for empathy are you need to have the presence of an affective state in oneself and you must be able to elicit your own affective (emotional) state by observing or imaging another person's affective state.

In other words, if you saw that I was upset then this observation of me being upset should result in you being upset as well.

<u>Related but different:</u>

Despite there being a lot of different emotions that are similar or related to empathy, each of the following is different from empathy in key ways.

- Mentalising- drawing inferences about another's mental state but empathy is about sharing affective state.
- Sympathy- refers to an emotional congruent with other people's feeling, but not necessarily strophic. Sympathy often entails a condescending quality to it.
- Emotion contagion- the tendency to automatically minimize and synchronic facial expressions vocalisation with these of another person and to converge emotionally.
- Empathic concern or compassion- similar to sympathy but involves motivation to act, so you want to do something about it.

Simulation theories:

These theories state that we come to understand others because of the activation of neural representation that responds to the states of others.

For example, to understand what others are doing, people stimulate their movements using our own movements.

In addition, to understand what others feel. We stimulate their feelings using our own emotions.

When we observe or imagine other people in pain; for replace; this will automatically activate the brain areas that are responsible for pain in our brain regions.

Measuring Empathy:

How do you measure an emotion such as Empathy?

This is difficult as an emotion isn't something that you can directly measure but there are methods that you can use to infer things about people's levels of empathy.

For example, you can use questionnaires to enquiry about people's emotions.

You can use brain imaging and other brain research methods, as discussed in Biological Psychology, to conduct research.

Although, there are a few specific types of questionnaires that exclusively looks at empathy called the Empathy Quotient (Baron-Cohen, 2004) and the Interpersonal Reactivity Index (Davis, 1983)

In addition, the Index is made up of a few components including:

- Perspective-taking- the tendency to spontaneously adopt the psychological point of view of others.
- Empathic concern- assess the other-oriented feeling of sympathy as well as concern for the unfortunate other.
- Personal distress- measures 'self-oriented' feeling of personal anxiety and unease intense interpersonal setting.
- Fantasy Scale – taps respondents' tendencies to transpose themselves imaginatively into the feelings and actions of fictitious characters in books, movies, and plays.

However, these questionnaires don't reflect modern definitions of empathy, but it's still interesting to consider.

CHAPTER 15: MIRROR NEURONS

The discovery of neurons is an exciting discovery that does spark a lot of interesting ideas as well as it has sparked a lot of controversies as well.

Originally, mirror neurons were found in monkeys because some of the neurons that are active when the monkey makes a movement are also activated when the monkey observes that movement done by someone else. (Di Pellegrino et al, 1992)

Although, mirrors neurons were found by mistake because the researchers found that the pain matrix; more specifically the Insula and anterior cingulate cortex; was involved in affective pain.

Therefore, these brain areas are involved when we feel the pain of others.

Empathy and mirror neurons:

Overall, the idea that mirror neurons are important for empathy is largely supported by evidence that focuses on imitating as well as observing facial expressions. These behaviours lead to the activation of areas that are typically associated with mirror neurons. For instance: the inferior frontal gyrus.

However, the evidence for mirror neurons in humans is largely indirect so it's hard to prove or disprove the concept of mirror neurons and empathy.

Additionally, there's no evidence in monkeys of mirror neurons in the somatosensory cortices or the insula. These are important brain regions for pain.

The empathy paradigm doesn't rely on observations of other's movement, so the definitive role of mirror neurons in empathy is questionable.

Finally, the term 'mirroring' should be seen as a loose analogy for either the stimulating or reproducing of the emotions of others in our own emotion-related neural system.

Empathy and autism:

There's substantial evidence that autistic individuals perform poorly or can't complete the false-belief tasks.

It's suggested that the theory of mind deficits are a

core feature of autism.

Please see <u>Development Psychology 2nd Edition</u> for more information on Theory of Mind.

Nevertheless, there's a lot of debate over this assumption because whilst deficits in theory of mind do exist in autistic individuals. They are not sufficient to explain this perceived condition. The idea that autistic people have impaired empathy is largely accepted in autism.

Although, the underlying causes are controversial and there's mixed evidence on stimulation and emotion sharing' empathy in autistic people.

Therefore, it's probably a combination of other processes that are probably better to explain these deficits. For example, self-other distinction or mentalising.

CHAPTER 15: EMOTION

Sitting down in the lecture theatre at the university, I remember this lecture well because of the interesting topic but mainly as a result of the traumatic lecturer.

We all felt bored by the end of the lecture because whilst the lecturer was passionate about the topic of emotion. She didn't engagingly present the 2 hour lecture and her PowerPoint didn't help much either. As there were 95 slides in the presentation and 75 of them were journal articles that she talked to us about.

Personally, I would have preferred the information straight up and maybe I would have looked up the articles in my own time.

In terms of this chapter, I only want to make this chapter easy to read and interesting for you.

Yet the first problem is how to see define emotion?

Definition of Emotion:

This is very difficult as what is emotion?

How can you explain what emotion is?

Well, one example of an attempted definition is when Buck (1998) said that emotions involve feelings, associated with expressive behaviours and have peripheral physiology responses.

In simpler words, emotions are feelings that are associated with behaviours and bodily responses.

Personally, I think that it's a good definition as it describes emotions well.

In addition, theories of emotion define emotion in terms of:

- Cognition
- Feelings
- Readiness for action

But what comes first?

The cognition then the feeling?

The feeling then the cognition?

Nobody truly knows for sure but several people have come up with some good theories over the centuries.

James-Lange theory:

Rather amazingly, two theorists came up with the exact same theory in the same year whilst being on two separate continents and not knowing each other.

This is called: the James- Lange theory that was proposed in 1884 saying that emotion is a production of the appropriate physiological responses and the appropriate behaviour.

Additionally, the theory proposes that the brain receives sensory feedback from the muscles to organs to produce emotion.

Meaning that the cognition or the feeling is produced after the bodily response as well as the feeling is the emotion.

Predictions:

However, if this theory is true then increasing the autonomic responses (bodily responses) should enhance emotion, as well as people with weaker responses should feel less emotion.

This is debated even now as some research supports this idea but other research doesn't.

So nobody knows if the theory is true or not.

Although, Bolnlium toxin therapy can lead to an increasingly positive mood by paralysing frowning muscles and this links to embodied social cognition. (Check out Sociocultural Psychology for more information)

This can potentially support this theory as it shows that by stopping the bodily response then it can have an impact on emotions.

Schachter and Singer's theory:

You can see the full case study and this theory in Biological Psychology but this theory proposes that "emotion is the result of contextual cues and physical cues that are combined with cognitive labelling.

In other words, emotion is the result of us labelling what's happening in the situation we're in and what our body is doing as well."

Source: Biological Psychology by Connor Whiteley

Canon-Bard theory:

This theory is of particular interest because unlike the theories before it, the Canon-Bard theory proposes that the emotional stimulus simultaneously triggers both the subjective emotional response (the feeling) and physiological response.

In other words, the arousal and the emotion occur at the same time.

Neural Basis for Emotion:

After looking at the theories of emotion, I wonder how does emotion occur in the body?

Is the brain involved?

The emotional brain:

Whilst most emotion is happening in the limbic system; other brain areas are involved.

For example, the amygdala; an almond-shaped structure from the Greek language, is very important for processing fear.

Building upon this the bodily is very clever as when we see something dangerous or fearful, the body sends the visual information about the threat to the visual thalamus who sends it to the amygdala as well as the brain area known as the visual cortex.

Nonetheless, only when it reaches the visual cortex does it become conscious.

The information being sent to the visual thalamus to the amygdala is important to survival as a response can be prepared before the threat reaches our conscious awareness.

Testosterone:

Whilst, I go into the topic of Aggression in more depth in Sociocultural Psychology, I have to at least mention aggression in an emotion chapter.

Therefore, aggression is closely linked to testosterone as men have higher levels of the hormone and they tend to engage in more aggressive behaviour than women.

Finally, testosterone leads to higher activation of the Amygdala.

A Quick Note on the Insula:

This brain area is where the emotion of disgust is localised as there is strongly activation of this area during the process of disgust.

Culture and Emotion:

As always I love culture and the impact that it has on human behaviour so Efren et al (1982) found that certain facial expressions were recognised across cultures as well as he found 6 basic emotions that were universal across all cultures: sad, contempt, happy, fear, shock and disgust.

However, it turned out that not all these emotions were universal and there were cultural influences in the way humans perceive emotion. Like: body language.

CHAPTER 16: CONSCIOUS

Originally, this topic was never meant to be in the book, but I stumbled across this topic in one of my many psychology textbooks and I thought:

"Well I may not have to learn this for my degree but maybe I'll learn something,"

And it turns out that I have and I constantly use the idea of the cognitive unconscious, but more on that later.

What is Consciousness?

Consciousness is our moment by moment awareness of ourselves, our environment and thoughts.

For example, conscious awareness of you being you, where you are and what you're thinking.

How do you study Conscious?

Again, I'll fully admit that the method in this section is very questionable as Freud popularised it but then the field of psychology dismissed it.

Nonetheless, I was surprised when I found out how useful this method could potentially be in certain situations.

Therefore, a method of studying consciousness is introspection. Whilst, it has its limits, it can still be informative.

Introspection is a process where we look inside ourselves to discover our thoughts, feelings and beliefs.

Whilst, introspection can be useful as a source of evidence and it's useful in a range of settings. It can be limited for a few reasons. For example:

- The inspector doesn't tell you what they're actually thinking.

This links to the social desirability bias where you give your answers in a certain way to reflect what's socially desirable.

- You might want to tell the truth, but you simply don't have the needed vocabulary.
- Another problem is when the inspector finds the right words, but the other person interprets it differently.

A terrible yet useful example is when an American says 'pants' but a British person thinks that they're talking about underwear.

The cognitive unconscious:

In addition, introspection is limited because it cannot tell us everything as the unconscious influences us in ways that we don't know about. Meaning that these unconscious influences can't be detected through introspection.

We use the term cognitive inference to describe certain aspects of human perception. For example, when you turn a corner and 'know' what's going to there is because your unconscious mind has inferred it.

Whereas, the cognitive unconscious is the term given to the mental support processes that exist outside our awareness. This process makes our perception, thinking and memory possible.

However, it must be noted that the cognitive unconscious is the term for these support processes and not the unconscious mind as described by Freud. This is because modern scholars strongly believe/know that the unconscious isn't an adversary of the conscious mind; like Freud proposed and the unconscious doesn't have its own desires or identities like Freud suggested.

Brain damage and unconscious functioning:

Knowing that the cognitive unconscious greatly limits introspection. This raises a few questions like:

- How much can our unconscious accomplish?
- What mental processes have to be done without conscious thought?

Some evidence to these questions can be found in people who have suffered brain damage.

As a result, people who suffer from anterograde amnesia, sadly have an inability to have conscious awareness. As in short, one study found sufferers couldn't remember a list of words consciously but after cues and hints they remembered the list.

Suggesting that the unconscious was involved.

Another interesting finding about the power of the unconscious functioning is that people that suffer from Blindsight; that's caused by having a brain lesion in the visual cortex; are for all practical purposes blind.

However, these people have an uncanny ability to reach towards or correctly 'guess' about objects in their visual field. Despite the patient or person say they are seeing nothing.

Isn't that amazing!

Mistaken introspection:

Nevertheless, introspection can sometimes be wrong.

A specific example of how introspection can be wrong is in Nisbelt and Wilson (1977) were shoppers told them that the preferred one nightgown over another because of the feel of the fabric. Despite the fabric being the same.

Function of consciousness:

The cognitive unconscious allows processes to happen that are fast, automatic as well as effortless. Thus, suggesting that the conscious is needed when we need to assert executive control over our thought processes.

For example, to raise above a habit or to resist something at the moment.

CHAPTER 17: THE BASIS OF CONSCIOUS

Neural basis for consciousness:

Regardless of research on consciousness and the cognitive unconscious. The fact remains that each of us has our set of inner experiences and we are all conscious.

The mind-body dual problem:

This problem focuses on the idea that the mind is a non-physical entity and the brain is a completely different physical entity. Yet these two entities seem to influence each other.

To answer this problem the philosopher Descartes thought the body influenced the soul and mind through the pineal gland. Whereas, modern scholars thought very differently.

Please Biological Psychology for more information.

Brain areas needed:

From studying people with 'reduced' consciousness. For example, people in comas or people who suffer from brain damage. We know that there are many different areas in the brain that seem to be crucial for consciousness, but this research has failed to locate a centre or a single major brain area for conscious.

As a result, conscious is compared to a light bulb that is turned on when we're conscious as well as changes its brightness depending on the mental state we're in.

The resulting area from this line of thinking has proposed two board categories of brain activity that are needed for two types of consciousness.

Firstly, you have our conscious awareness for our level of sensitivity or alertness. For instance, thinking quickly about an idea or memory is the low level. Whereas, focusing on the stimuli makes us more alter.

Secondly, you have the context for our conscious. For example, when we're thinking about the past, we use our cortical structures in the forebrain. But when we think about tasks in front of us, we use the cortical features in our visual system.

Hence, showing how the needed brain areas differ depending on the type of conscious we require.

Neural correlates of consciousness:

These are specific brain areas that seem to relate to a person's conscious experience.

For example, when we look at faces neuroimaging tells us that there's higher than normal activation of the fusiform face in the brain.

In addition, when we look at houses. There's higher than normal activation in the parahippocampus place are.

Therefore, showing us how certain brain areas correlate with different types of consciousness.

Global workspace hypothesis:

According to this hypothesis, our conscious is possible as a result of patterns of integrated neural activity that's made possible by the 'workspace' neurons.

In addition, these workspace neurons are controlled by our attention.

In other words, this hypothesis proposes that we're conscious because of the unique neural activity that is created by the workspace neurons as well as consciousness can be increased or decreased depending on the amount of attention, we give a particular stimulus.

Finally, whilst this hypothesis is purely speculative, it does explain many aspects of consciousness. Such as it's functions.

PART FIVE: LANGUAGE

CHAPTER 18: LANGUAGE

Considering my late language development, I truly love language and despite my occasional stuttering, I still push on through and I talk.

My love for language is one of the reasons why I became an author of both psychology as well as sci-fi fantasy books.

But the interesting questions are: what is a language and what is a language made from?

<u>What is language?</u>

A language is a human communication either spoken or written and it consists of the use and interpretation of words in a structured and conventional way.

For example, English is a language because you can understand this book as these words and characters are arranged in a structured and conventional way that gives it meaning.

In addition, our use of language makes us different from most other species. As supported by Petitto and Seidenberg (1979) managed to get chimpanzees to learn bits and pieces of language.

Although, the chimpanzees didn't use or understand the language as they only used it to get something from their caretakers rather than trying to truly express thought and meaning.

Although, our ability to talk about the past, present and future, not there and hypothetical things makes our language different from other species.

Also, there are about 5,000-6,000 languages worldwide and most languages have many dialects.

Interestingly, there's an infinite number of combinations that can be produced in a language from a finite number of letters as a language has rules of form.

Finally, language is a universal behaviour as all cultures have their own language, but all languages share some universal features of structure.

Structure of language:

Language is made up of a number of different components that are important.

Phonemes:

Phonemes are the sound of a letter.

For example, 'pat' vs 'bat' with the difference between the two words being the sound of the letter p and b.

In addition, humans can arrange letters is different ways as well as the human speech apparatus can produce hundreds of different sounds clearly and reliability.

Interestingly, each language makes systematic use of only a small possible number of these sounds.

Basically, each language refines the system of phonemes as at birth we can produce all phonemes but over the course of our first year. We refine the system according to our own language.

Morphemes:

Another component of language is morphemes and these are the smallest unit of meaning in a language, with there being about 40 of these units in English.

For instance, Boys can be broken down into boy (content morpheme) and 's' (function morpheme)

Although, function morpheme cannot stand alone but they can change the meaning of a word.

Phrases, sentences, and Syntax:

Finally, the last component of a language and the most well-known are phrases and sentences.

Such as: English has an analytic structure that relies on word order to convey meaning.

This is referred to as Syntax. A combination of words that follow the rules of grammar.

Ambiguity:

Although, syntax might help with understanding. There can still be a lot of ambiguity in a language.

One example is the English language that has a lot of ambiguity.

Like: Time flies like an arrow.

1. Literal meaning
2. Time Flies (a name for an insect) like an arrow.
3. Time (person's name) flies like an arrow.

Leading us to question, how do we get meaning from words?

Definitional theory of word meaning:

This theory argues that words are represented in our minds. Like: they are in a dictionary as well as each word has a category.

For example, tree, flower, and bush are all plants.

Nevertheless, something can be a member of many different categories.

For example, a tree could be a part of the plant and organic category.

Despite all this about the theory, it's too simplistic and I doubt that anyone remembers definitions of each and every word.

Because if we could then surely it would be a lot easier than it actually is to define simple words like: 'the'?

Prototype theory of meaning: (Rosch, 1973)

Leading us onto the slightly better theory of the Prototype Theory of Meaning that argues that we store a mental image of that category. This is the prototype.

Subsequently, we determine a category by comparing things to the representation of the category.

For instance, we know what a tree should look like

then we use that knowledge to compare other items against it to determine if it's a tree.

In addition, the category that we have in our minds is an Idea example of the category and our prototype may have a combination of features of various members of category as well as it doesn't actually need to be a real thing.

One example of this is we imagine a cat to have fur and four legs, but when we see a creature that isn't furry and only has three legs. We can compare this creature to our mental prototype to determine that it probably isn't a cat.

Research Support:

Finally, both theories quite a bit of supporting research as well as Armstrong et al (1983) argued both theories help us to understand a word.

CHAPTER 19: HOW DO WE LEARN A LANGUAGE?

After looking at what a language is and what a language is made up of, how do we learn a language?

Social origins:

As always all behaviours are a mixture of environmental factors and biological factors. Therefore, in terms of environmental factors, Social Learning Theory plays a role in language development. This is because the child can watch a model to learn language.

Interestingly, Fernald (1992) found that new-borns heart rates quickened when they heard a positive toned voice.

Environmental factors:

Building upon the social origins of language more, environmental factors are vital as a parent's use of

Child direct speech (CDS) or motherese and parentese are vital for language development.

(You know the voice that you only use for babies or children)

Furthermore, Skinner (1957) proposed that there's a critical period for language development as if you don't learn a language by the age of 5 then it's very difficult to become fluent in a language.

Although, environmental factors aren't the only way of learning a language as deaf infants also babble, suggesting innate factors are involved.

Chomsky:

For example, Chomsky proposed that humans have an innate language acquisition device (LAD) and this device enables children to learn a language before device deactivates after a critical period.

This is because the brain is hardwired to learn a language.

However, this section is simply an introduction that will be expanded upon in my book, Developmental Psychology 2nd Edition.

Language and thought:

For a while now, there have been a few different arguments that our language impacts our thoughts and I once took part in a piece of psychology research that looked at Whorf's hypothesis.

Some of these arguments include:

- Vygotsky- thought and language develop independently then become connected.
- Paiget- thoughts come before language.
- Whorf's linguistic relativity- your language directly or heavily influences your thinking.

Overall, I thought that the Whorfian hypothesis is very interesting because the experiment I took part in looking at the differences between the English, French and Dutch language and how they describe the position of objects as each of these languages have their own way of describing an object's position.

Linguistic relativism:

In short, the language we speak affects the manner we perceive and think about the world, and this directly impacts how encodes categories of objects in our language.

For example, The Hopi Tribe has no past tense, so Whorf said that they don't think about the past.

Areas of the brain:

In terms of brain areas that are important for language, it is mainly the left hemisphere that it's important.

However, the following lobes are important and have different roles to play in language:

- Parietal- speaking word
- Frontal- generating word
- Temporal- hearing words
- Occipital- seeing words

Nonetheless, the Broca area that organises words into articulated speech as well as Wernicke area that is important for the comprehension of spoken words; are important as well.

Interestingly, when it comes to language and which hemisphere is the most important for language 90% of right-handed people use their left hemisphere.

Whereas left-handed people are more bilateral or right lateralisation.

Although, understanding emotion in words is in the right hemisphere for both types of people.

Personally, I definitely think that that's weird.

Bibliography:

Lee Parker (author), Darren Seath (author) Alexey Popov (author), *Oxford IB Diploma Programme: Psychology Course Companion,* 2nd edition, OUP Oxford, 2017

Alexey Popov, *IB Psychology Study Guide: Oxford IB Diploma Programme,* 2nd edition, OUP Oxford, 2018

https://www.thinkib.net/psychology/page/22420/localization-plasticity

First accessed on 15th March 2019

https://mrseplinibpsychologyclassblog.wordpress.com/2017/12/08/schachter-singer-1962

First accessed on 15th March 2019

Eysenck, M. W., & Keane, M. T. (2015). Cognitive psychology: A student's handbook. Psychology press.

Gleitman, H., Gross, J., & Reisberg, D. (2011) Psychology (8th International Student Edition). London: W.W. Norton.

GET YOUR FREE 8 PSYCHOLOGY BOOK BOXSET USING THE LINK BELOW

https://www.subscribepage.com/psychology boxset

Thank you for reading.

I hoped you enjoyed it.

If you did, please consider leaving an honest review as this helps with the discoverability of the book and I very much appreciate it.

If you want a FREE book and keep up to date about new books and project. Then please sign up for my newsletter at www.connorwhiteley.net/

Have a great day.

About the author:

Connor Whiteley is the author of over 20 books in the sci-fi fantasy, nonfiction psychology and books for writer's genre and he is a Human Branding Speaker and Consultant.

He is a passionate warhammer 40,000 reader, psychology student and author.

Who narrates his own audiobooks and he hosts The Psychology World Podcast.

All whilst studying Psychology at the University of Kent, England.

Also, he was a former Explorer Scout where he gave a speech to the Maltese President in August 2018 and he attended Prince Charles' 70th Birthday Party at Buckingham Palace in May 2018.

Plus, he is a self-confessed coffee lover!

Please follow me on:

Website: www.connorwhiteley.net

Twitter: @scifiwhiteley

Please leave on honest review as this helps with the discoverability of the book and I truly appreciate it.

Thank you for reading. I hope you've enjoyed.

All books in 'An Introductory Series':

Biological Psychology 2nd Edition

Cognitive Psychology 2nd Edition

Sociocultural psychology- 2nd edition

Abnormal Psychology 2nd Edition

Psychology of Human Relationships- 2nd Edition

Developmental Psychology 2nd Edition

Health Psychology

Research in Psychology

A guide to mental health and treatment around the world- A Global look at depression

Forensic Psychology

Other books by Connor Whiteley:

The Angel of Return

The Angel of Freedom

Garro: Galaxy's End

Garro: Rise of the Order

Garro: End Times

Garro: Short Stories

Garro: Collection

Garro: Heresy

Garro: Faithless

Garro: Destroyer of Worlds

Garro: Collections Book 4-6

Winter's Coming

Winter's Hunt

Winter's Revenge

Companion guides:

Biological Psychology 2nd Edition Workbook

Cognitive Psychology 2nd Edition Workbook

Sociocultural Psychology 2nd Edition Workbook

Abnormal Psychology 2nd Edition Workbook

Psychology of Human Relationships 2nd Edition Workbook

Health Psychology Workbook

Forensic Psychology Workbook

Audiobooks by Connor Whiteley:

Biological Psychology

Cognitive Psychology

Sociocultural Psychology

Abnormal Psychology

Psychology of Human Relationships

Health Psychology

Developmental Psychology

Research in Psychology

Forensic Psychology

Garro: Galaxy's End

Garro: Rise of The Order

Garro: Short Stories

Garro: End Times

Garro: Collection

Business books:

Time Management: A Guide for Students and Workers

Leadership: What Makes a Good Leader? A Guide for Students and Workers.

Business Skills: How to Survive the Business World? A Guide for Students, Employees and Employers.

Business Collection

GET YOUR FREE BOOK AT:
WWW.CONNORWHITELEY.NET